PICTURE A HOME RUN

A Baseball Drawing Book

by Anthony Wacholtz

illustrated by Erwin Haya

CAPSTONE PRESS
a capstone imprint

TABLE OF CONTENTS

Take Me Out to the Ball Game (to Draw!)

It's time to step up to the plate and start drawing! Learn some tips and draw yourself into the action on the baseball field. Are you ready to smash a mammoth home run? Or would you rather dive headfirst into second with a stolen base? Maybe you'd like to deliver the pitch that wins the World Series. Why not draw them all?

Follow the simple step-by-step drawings in this book, and you'll be on your way to baseball stardom. Before you know it, you'll be part of the game. Let's get started!

Before you head out on the field, grab some supplies:

1. First you'll need drawing paper. Any type of blank, unlined paper will do.

2. Pencils are the easiest to use for your drawing projects. Make sure you have plenty of them.

3. It's easier to make clean lines with sharpened pencils. Keep a pencil sharpener close by.

4. As you practice drawing, you'll need a good eraser. Pencil erasers wear out very quickly. Get a rubber or kneaded eraser.

5. When your drawing is finished, you can trace over it with a black ink pen or a thin felt-tip marker. The dark lines will make your drawing jump off the page.

6. If you decide to color your drawings, colored pencils and markers usually work best. You can also use colored pencils to shade your drawings and make them more lifelike.

PATIENCE AT THE PLATE

Here comes the pitch! You have a split second to decide what to do. Are you going to take a swing or hold off for a better pitch?

MAKING CONTACT

You were waiting for it: a belt-high fastball down the middle. You bring the bat around and feel the ball squarely hit the barrel. This ball's going for a ride!

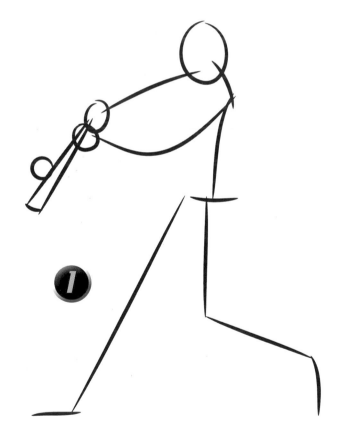

1

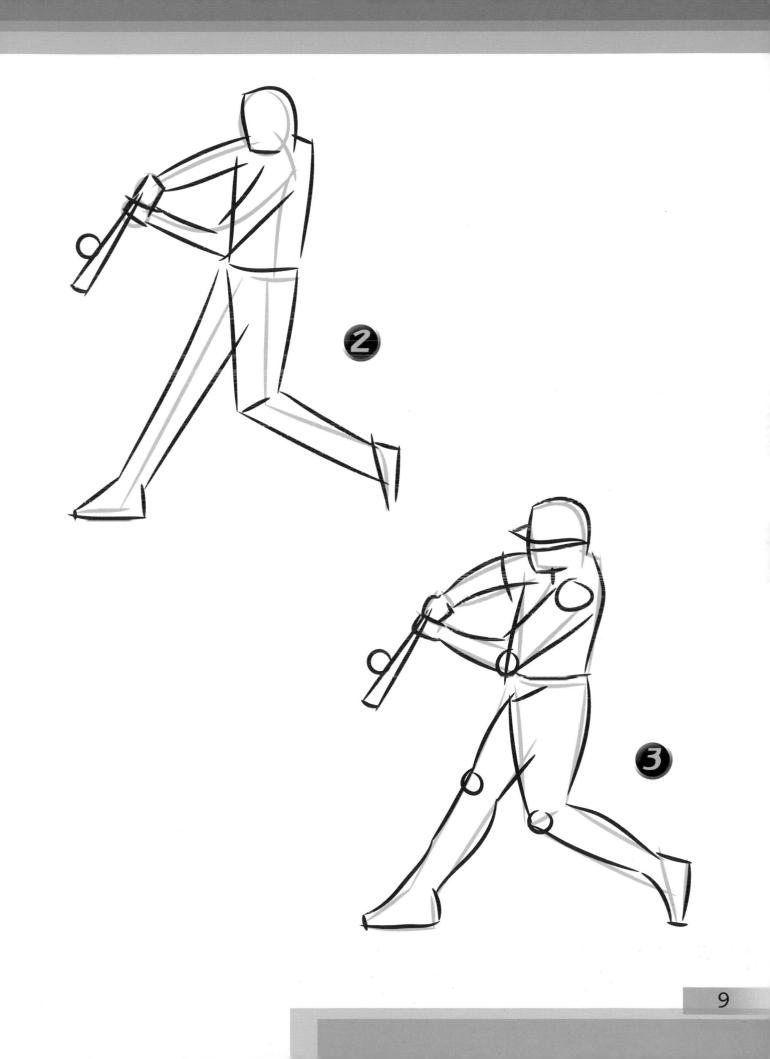

Home Run

Crack! You watch the ball soar after a mighty swing. Nothing left to do but start your home run trot!

1

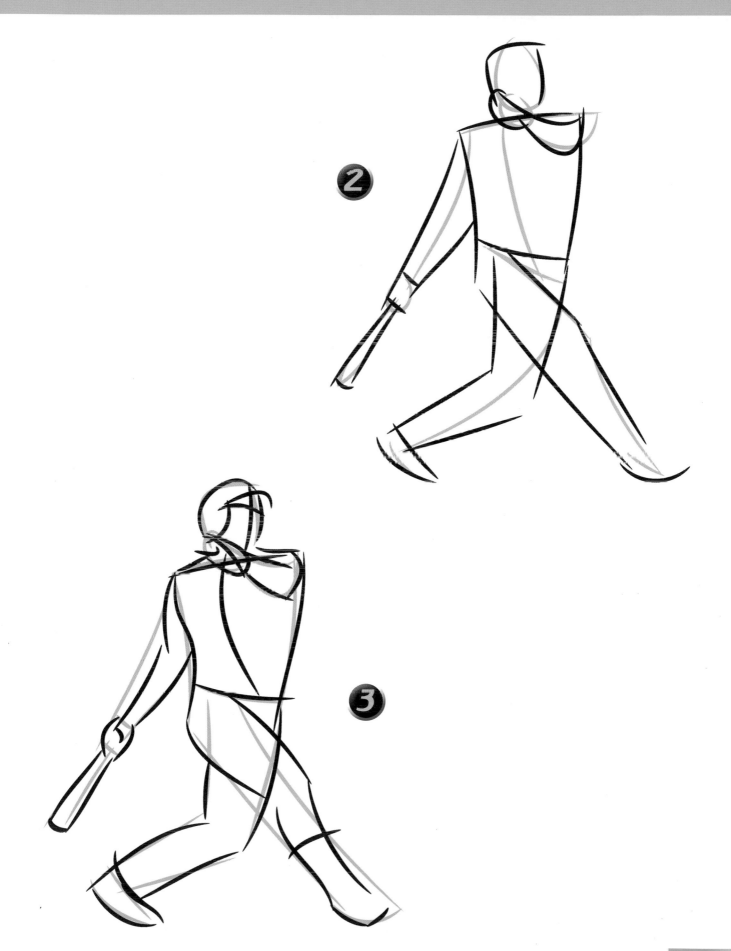

SQUARING UP TO BUNT

Here comes the pitch! You set yourself to bunt so you can advance the runner. With a little luck, you may be able to get on base yourself!

1

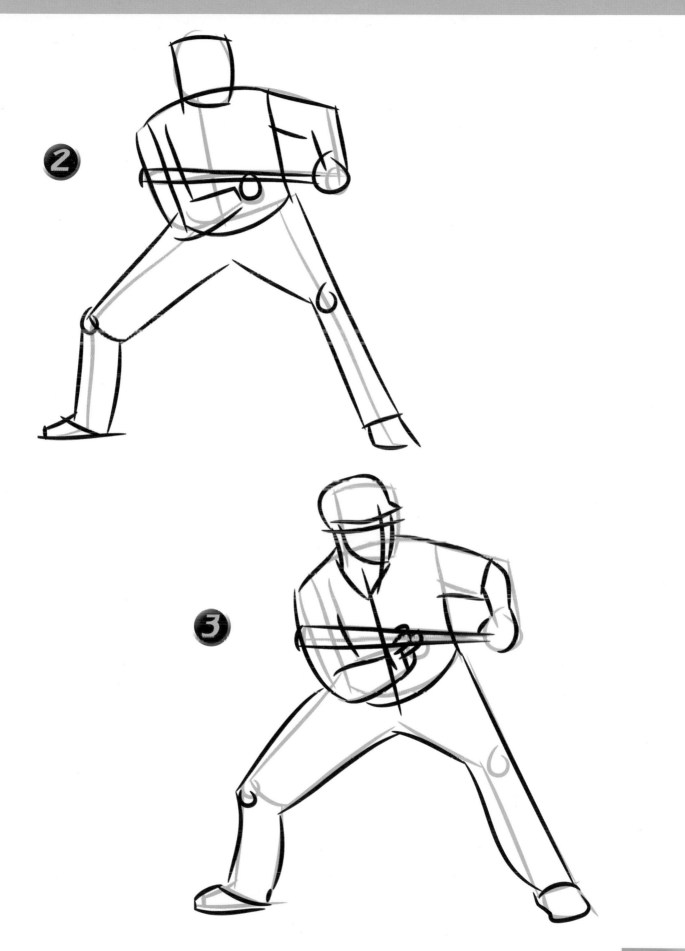

DIG FOR THIRD

A deep fly ball to the gap! You round second base with your arms pumping. It's going to be a close play at third!

1

STEALING BASES

The pitcher didn't pay attention to you, and now you're going to make him pay. With a headfirst dive, you slide into second base. Did you beat the throw?

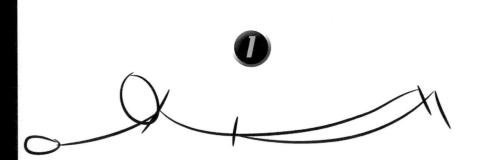

1

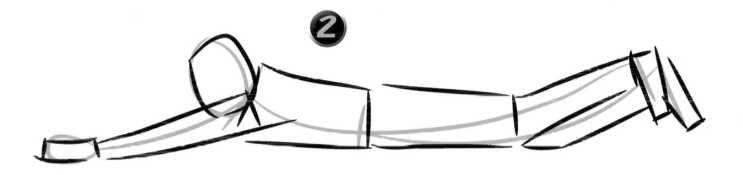

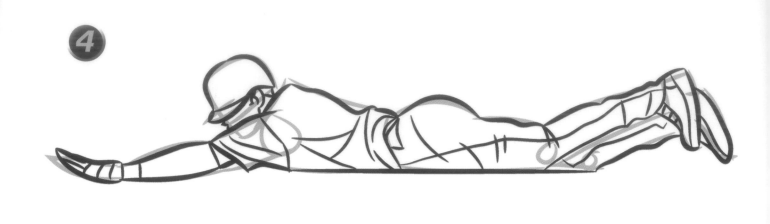

④

STAY IN FRONT

Crouched down, legs apart, two hands on the ball. There's no way this grounder's getting past you!

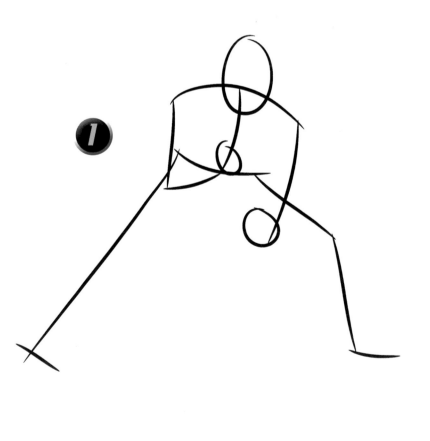

1

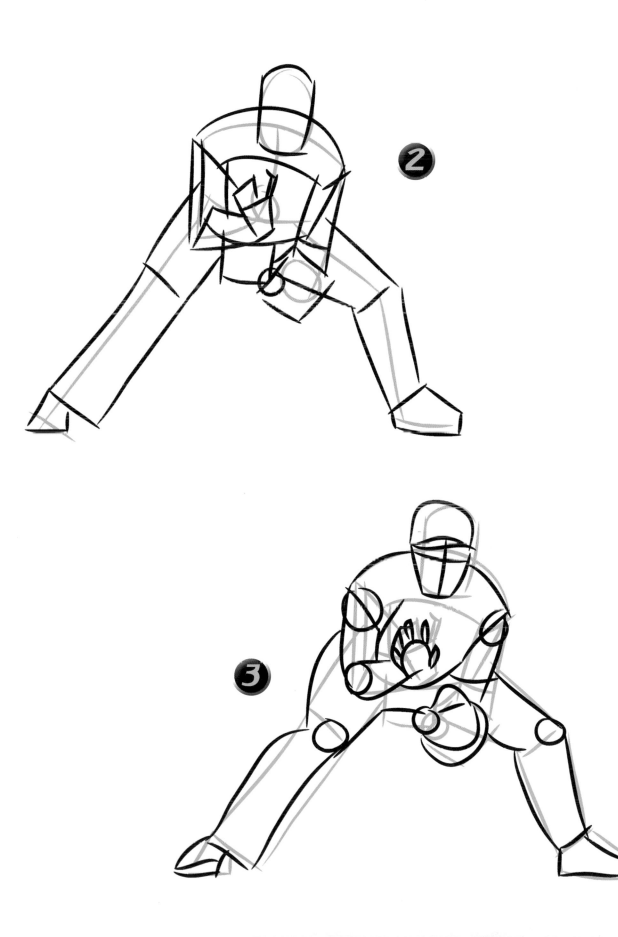

MAKE THE THROW

You've fielded the ball, but that's only half the play. You plant your feet and cock your arm back to throw. You'll have to fire the ball to first to beat the runner and get the out!

STRETCH FOR THE OUT

You know the throw is going to be close, so you stretch your arm out and get ready. You feel the thump of the ball in your glove just before the runner crosses first base. He's out!

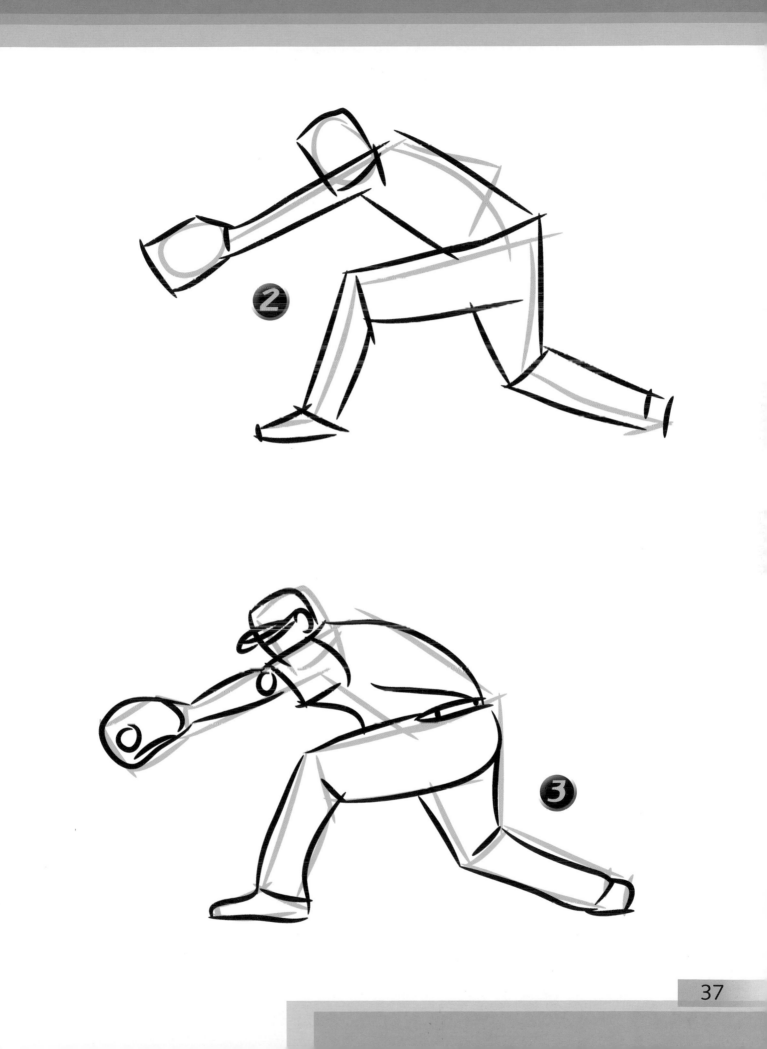

Down the Line

The ball jumps off the bat and screams down the left field line. With lightning-fast reflexes, you leap toward the ball with your arm extended. What a play!

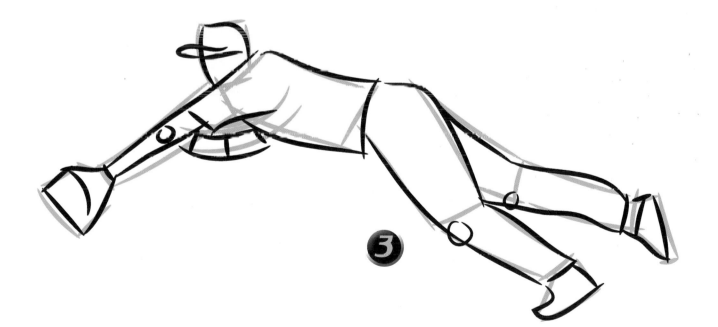

PLAY AT THE PLATE

Here comes the relay! The throw is right on target. It's up to you to make the catch and tag out the runner!

1

DOUBLE THE OUTS

The shortstop lobs the ball to you as you step on second. Spinning in midair, you fire off a quick throw to the first baseman. Double play!

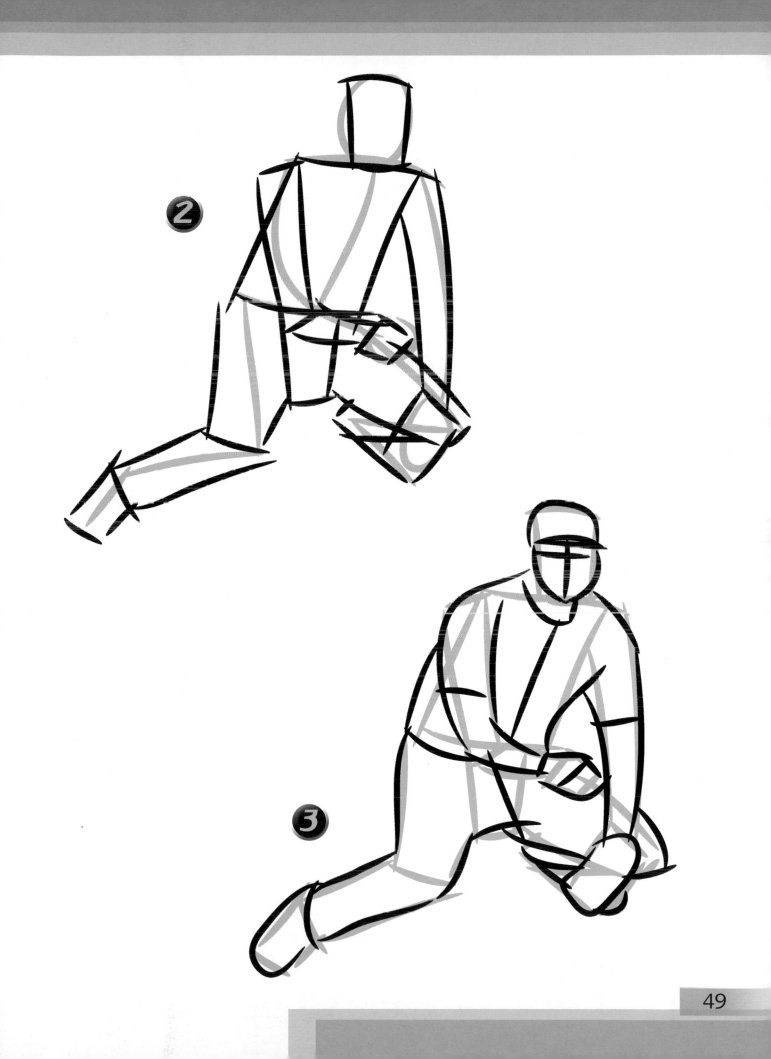

ROBBING HOMERS

A deep fly ball sends the other team into a cheering frenzy. But it's not gone yet! You scale the wall and reach back with your glove. You can't wait to see the instant replay!

1

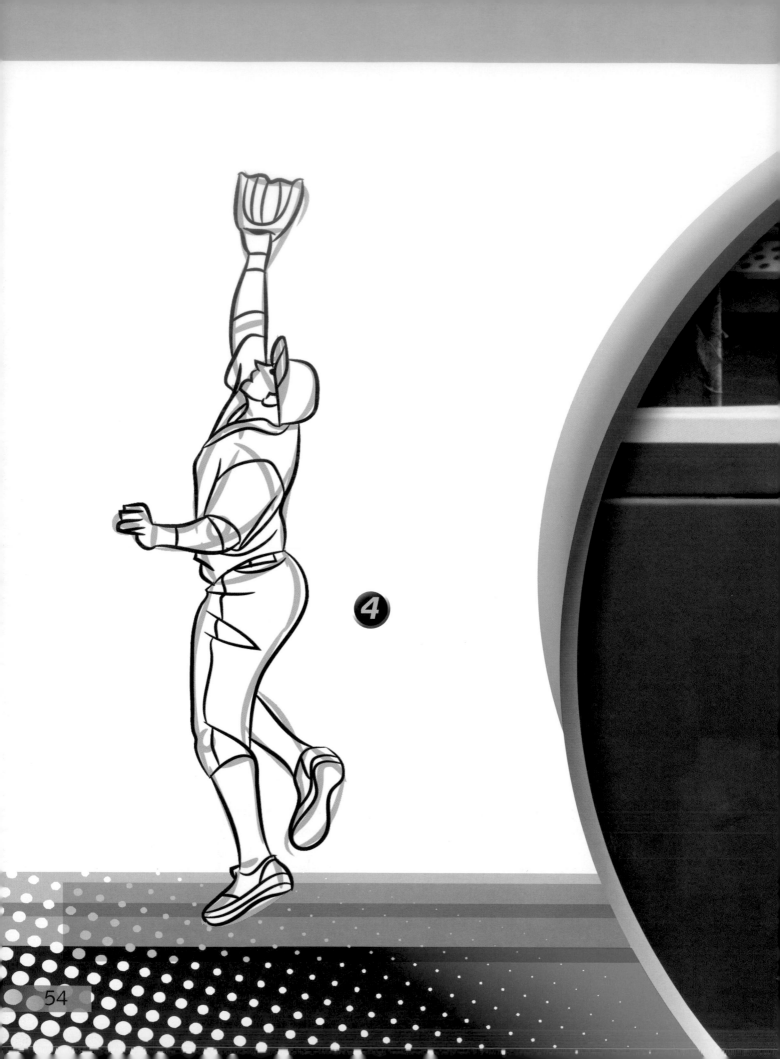

THE WINDUP

The catcher gives you the sign. After checking the runners, you go through your windup and release the pitch. The moment it leaves your fingers, you know it's a strike.

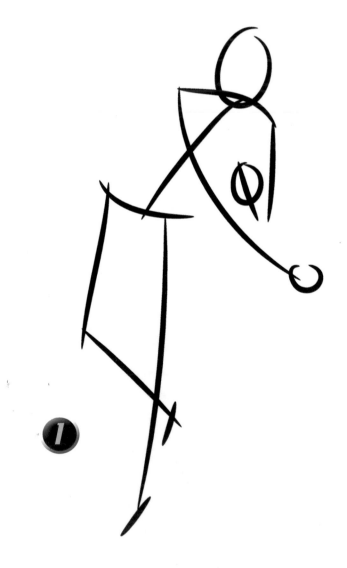

1

SPECIAL DELIVERY

You've kept the batter guessing, and you're a strike away from winning the game. Can you get one more pitch past the batter?

READ MORE

Ames, Lee J. *Draw 50 Athletes: The Step-by-Step Way to Draw Wrestlers and Figure Skaters, Baseball and Football Players, and Many More.* 2nd ed. New York: Watson-Guptill, 2012.

Dreier, David. *Baseball: How It Works.* Sports Illustrated Kids. Mankato, Minn.: Capstone Press, 2010.

Wacholtz, Anthony. *The Ultimate Collection of Pro Baseball Records.* Sports Illustrated Kids. Mankato, Minn.: Capstone Press, 2013.

INTERNET SITES

FactHound offers a safe, fun way to find Internet sites related to this book. All of the sites on FactHound have been researched by our staff.

Here's all you do:

Visit *www.facthound.com*

Type in this code: 9781476531069

Drawing with Sports Illustrated Kids is published by Capstone Press, 1710 Roe Crest Drive, North Mankato, Minnesota 56003
www.capstonepub.com

Library of Congress Cataloging-in-Publication Data
Wacholtz, Anthony.
    Picture a home run : a baseball drawing book / by Anthony Wacholtz.
    pages cm.—(Sports illustrated kids. Drawing with sports illustrated kids)
    ISBN 978-1-4765-3106-9 (library binding)
    1. Home runs (Baseball)—Juvenile literature. I. Title.
GV868.4.W33 2014
796.357'26—dc23   2013006659

TITLES IN THIS SERIES:

A Baseball Drawing Book

A Basketball Drawing Book

A Hockey Drawing Book

A Football Drawing Book

Editorial Credits
Tracy Davies McCabe, designer; Eric Gohl, media researcher; Eric Manske, production specialist

Photo Credits
Sports Illustrated: Al Tielemans, 15, 31, 35, Bob Rosato, 46–47, Chuck Solomon, 26–27, Damian Strohmeyer, 43, David E. Klutho, cover, 59, John Biever, 7, 19, 23, 39, 55, 63, John W. McDonough, 51, Robert Beck, 11

Printed in the United States of America in North Mankato, Minnesota.
032013   007223CGF13